Obscured Passages

A Memoir in Verse of Child Trafficking
& the Resilience of the Human Mind

Nichole M. Willden

To anyone who had their voice
silenced by people who should
have listened,

I wrote this for you.

 Contents

Then: The Holy Josephic Priesthood.. 1

Now: Nightmares... 2

Then: Shh! Shh! Shh!.. 4

Now: Crazy... 5

Then: Fine... 7

Now: Voices... 9

Then: Whore.. 11

Now: Visions... 14

Then: Needy.. 17

Now: Depressed.. 19

Then: Attention... 21

Now: Movie... 24

Then: Dark... 28

Now: The Shelf... 31

Then: Blessed.. 33

Now: Are We Okay?... 38

Then: Silent..40

Now: Alyss...42

Then: Bare Feet.. 45

Now: Silent..48

Then: Pain and Blood...50

 Contents

Now: Drowning.. 54

Then: Beth.. 57

Now: Invisible.. 62

Then: Rabid Dogs.. 64

Now: Neediest... 66

Then: Invisible... 68

Now: Obscured Passages...................................... 69

Then: Replaced.. 71

Now: To Be.. 73

Then: Happy.. 74

Now: Headspace.. 77

Then: School Library... 80

Now: The Door... 82

Then: Counting.. 83

Now: Library.. 87

Then: Unobscured... 90

Now: Home.. 94

Then: Move.. 96

Now: Family... 99

Then: The Plane... 102

Now: Now.. 106

A Note from the Author

Content Warning

This is a true story about my early childhood experiences in a cult. Although I write in poetry form, the beauty ends there. This book is not an easy journey. It includes topics surrounding sexual abuse, torture, physical abuse, emotional abuse and manipulation, psychological abuse, indoctrination, slavery, religious abuse, cult rites and prayers, denial, neglect, and human trafficking. While I do not go into descriptive detail about all acts, the allusion to them is heavily pronounced throughout this work. Enter with care.

Then The Holy Josephic Priesthood

I am a Virgin of the High Josephic Priesthood
walking the path of the righteous.

Obedience and sweetness
drape my shoulders and veil my head.

Swaddled and enfolded in a blanket of specialness,
I keep my eyes on the ground.

"You're like a princess," I'm told in a whisper.

I'm anointed.

I'm appointed
to be someone's Virgin wife.
For only tonight.

"You're a beautiful bride."

The white drape over my face leads me to believe them.
I am beautiful. I am a Virgin.
I am Blessed and Special and Sacred.

I am six years old.

Nightmares

I wake with a gasp,
grasping onto the last vestiges of terror.

I feel the cloth on my skin. I feel the warm breath
against my neck.
I feel the hands upon my head,
pressing down,
a blessing of silence and shame.
They say my name.

And I am thrashing around
in my adulthood,
kicking and screaming as I never could do as a child.

I am wild with fear
and injustice. I don't trust this
to pass. But it does. I relax.

A little.

I am grown.
I'm alone
and nothing is touching me.
Not even my blankets, which have fallen to the floor.

I am not a little girl anymore.

The fear passes. There's a lapse,
and I wonder, *What was I afraid of?*

My nightmares tell me lies.
They try to tell me that *something happened*
        but I roll my eyes.

Because nothing happened.

I would remember.

 Then   Shh! Shh! Shh!

"Remember to be silent."

Mommy doesn't know I'm a bride.

My fingers count the secrets I am holding inside.

Tap-tap-tap: My fingers on the mattress.

She will be blessed if I am blessed.

Tap-tap-tap.

The smell of his hand over my mouth
—my husband tonight—
fills my heart with terror but also relief that I will bring blessings and joy
to Mommy—
who is so sad.

Tap-tap-tap.

I can make her feel better.
I can help God bless her.
I can show how much I love her
through my sweetness and obedience.

Tap-tap-tap.

"Shh!" he says and encloses my tapping fingers in his fist.

Shh! Shh! Shh!
Blessings come
in the silence.

Crazy

"I don't know why I keep
dreaming of this silence,
this overwhelming darkness.
I am buried under it but also floating
above it.

> I am on both sides
> of a closed door.
> On the outside, I lift my fist
> but am afraid to knock.
> On the inside, I wait, breathless,
> for any reason to walk through.

I feel trapped
but also like all I have to do
is turn around and I'll be free.
I don't know…"
Maybe I'm crazy.

My therapist smiles like she knows
my thoughts. Even though I have always been
an expert at hiding
what I truly think.

Somehow, she sees more
than I ever thought
I would show. She seems
to know
that I'm crazy.

"What do you think you need?"

What

    a

        ridiculous

            question!

I don't *need* things.
Need
is
dangerous.
It is vulnerable.
It is hungry dogs slavering at my feet
while I walk away, not quite fast enough.

I can't *need* or

I'll

be

b-r-e-a-k-a-b-l-e.

I can't be breakable.

If I am a flower in a pot,
I have been starved and drowned intermittently.
The sun is always
too far away,
but I learned how to survive
without it.

"Nothing. I'm fine."

I am always
fine.

Then   Fine

"You are fine!"
His voice is a roaring ocean,
        a sharpened blade.

I stifle
my
tears
with the heel of my hands,
rub my nose against the inside of my arm.

I *think* I am in pain.
I *think* I am hurt.
I *think* I am crying
        because he hurt me.

But I am wrong.

His voice
is a song
I know the lyrics to already.

"I'm fine," I say, choking on my tears. I swallow them down. "I am
fine."

"Good girl," he replies, and I know then
that I was wrong.
He did not hurt me.
He *would* not hurt
one of the Virgins
of the Lord.
I
must have been
mistaken.

Kids are wrong a lot.
We are
only
learning.

He is a grown man who knows
                                        all the things.

It stings to remember
I doubted him.
I don't have a right to doubt
the Priests
of the Holy Josephic Priesthood.
They are all
Good.

And I am a bad girl for crying when I'm fine.

"Sorry," I whisper.

"It's all right," he says.
"Close your eyes."

                I am tumbling
                                away from him
                                                in my mind.

And I'm just
fine.

Voices

I'm talking to the voices again.
Not *real*, audible voices.
They're just in my head.
Are we okay? they ask again.
Is it me?
Or is it them?
Either way, the question is always the same:
Are we okay?

No.
I know I'm not
because the tears flow
freely down my face.

I'm in darkness.

Night has fallen
and I'm driving a long, dark road.
No one is here
to ease the silence. Except the voices.
The voices that probably mean I'm crazy,
  even though they're only in my mind.
  The voices that talk not just to me,
  but to each other.

No. An echo in the darkness.
We are not okay.

We are walking in a long hallway,
approaching a door
that was shut, locked,
and barricaded.

Uh-uh. Don't go there.

The sternest voice tells me
to walk away.
He always wants me to walk
away
from the door
beyond which is an answer to my sadness.

Is there an answer to sadness?

Probably not. But it's worth a shot.

Mom was sad and that never stopped.

True enough.
But I'm not her.
I was never, ever her.

I keep driving, my eyes on the road.
I keep straining toward the barricaded door.

I'm getting close now.

Then **Whore**

I'm close
to dangerous
consequences.

I know it's wrong to look at the
Highest Priest's eyes. But I can't help
sneaking a peek while
he's glaring
down at me.

I've been delivered to him
by my husband,
who said sweet things
while passing
my hand to this holiest of men.

But *his* hand squeezes too tightly.
I know the sweet
things my husband said do not
mean as much as the
condemning words, "She cried."

It's a sin as deep as lies,
as deep as refusal
or disobedience.

I'm a naughty girl, that handhold claims.
And his angry eyes
repeat
what I already know:
no blessings for me tonight.

The black robe walks away;
our bond of marriage
breaks
as soon as he closes the door.

"Are you a Whore?" the High Priest asks.

I shake my head.
But there's a part of me that whispers,
Yes.

"Only the
Whores of the Earth
need to cry in the arms
of the Priesthood.
Only the Whores!"

I go over his knee
and am staring
down
at the stone-cold ground.
"Because the Whores
will all be found!" his voice thunders. "They hide
among the clean and righteous daughters."
His hand beats his fury
against my bottom.
My face turns red, but I press my lips together
and won't let myself whine.
Whores cry, I tell myself.

But the High Priest's hand is firmer than my resolve.
It keeps coming
over and over.
And when the tears fall,
        I am filled with terror…

                        Maybe I really am a Whore after all.

"I'm sorry!" I scream.

But he doesn't believe me.
He stands me upright
and smacks my face.

"Whores will suffer in the dark!"
God's voice must be
like a dragon,
because His Priest's voice is a lion.
threatening
to tear me apart.

But then I'm surrounded by dark.
The cabinet door
slams
shut, and I huddle
on the splintery wooden floor.
I know this place.
I've been here
before.
And I know the only way to get out
is to prove
I am pure.

Visions

Sometimes in bed at night I have visions I am someone else entirely.
- I am *not* a needy girl from a broken home.
- I am *not* depressed enough that my lethargy stretches the length of an ocean and my tears are the weight of a running river.
- I am *not* a girl who was duped by her religion for several decades.
- I am *not* the fattest person in any room.
- I am *not* too passionate, too outspoken, too needy.

Needy.

Needy.

But most of all,
- I am *not, not, not* gay

I am swept away
to a room full of books. It's a place where I am free
to imagine.

An authoritative man tells me what to do, and I am happy to do it.
I am a wife and have the life I always planned to have.
A child on each hip and one holding me by the hand.
No, of course, I do not work.
And I imagine a wealthy man, somehow, even though if this was my reality, I would have married a child barely finished with college and without a penny.
But in my vision, he owns a home,
and I am inside it with all his babies.

A piece of me gags on the sweetness of the dream.

Not the sweetness, a scathing voice screams, *the grossness. This is not a dream. It's an archaic nightmare that steals your voice and all your autonomy.*

It's what I was born for. To be
some man's
    quiet
    wife.
But that's not
how it worked out.
I was never what
the "righteous" men
wanted: small, blond, and petite.

I was always the size of a
             thousand
                 broken
                     promises.

I was always the last
flower plucked from the wall
when the dancers were all
implored to find
a partner.

And now I know
the truth.
I am gay.

I am a spray of rainbows
and flying banners.

I am a clock ticking itself off a mantle.

Homophobia is a cancer
that tries to destroy me
from the inside out.

This is not the way a loving God created you.

My eyes roll and I roll over
to snub myself.
The part of myself that still believes
there could possibly be
a God in this powder keg of chaos.

But why is your dream always to become some man's quiet slave?

"It's late," I say and sigh away the question. Again.

Are we okay?

Then   Needy

I'm not okay.

I'm twenty.
I have my mom on the phone,
but she's not happy.
Not with her family.
Not with life.
And especially
not with me.

"You're my neediest child."

I'm blindsided
by her truth.
And her truth is probably the real truth. The "everyone" truth.
The reason
I am alone
even though I am so old.

Confusing words from nowhere whisper in my brain, Whores cry.

I swallow
down
the impulse to let
tears fall. I try again to be a wall.
To be small.
Let her words bounce off. Let myself be stone.

"Oh."

It didn't work.
She definitely knows she's wounded me.
She tries to backtrack with "Well, I just mean…"

"I know what you mean."

We get off the phone
and I know I won't call her again.
Not if I'm desperate.
Not even
if death
is the only
other
option.

I would rather die than be needy.

Not *just* needy.

The neediest.

Her neediest child.

I might die anyway.
From shame.
Whores cry.
Again the words that
bring no comfort
when tears course down my face.

Depressed

I'm crying. Again.
I wish it was as comfortable as a book
that falls open to a favorite page.
But it's not.
Crying is opening a hard-shell coconut with only a rock.
Crying is putting on a bra that doesn't quite fit and has pinching
underwire.
Crying is a pack of growling dogs, snarling and defending what they
perceive as their territory.

"Something is troubling you." My therapist, ever calm and patient.

I deny it with a shake of my head. I cling to a pillow, hug it tightly to my
chest.
"I'm just depressed."

I have always been depressed.
My mom and I discussed that it started at the divorce.
When my dad decided to stay
three states away
from his family starting fresh
in an unfinished house.

But I know better.
I was depressed before that.

When my mom told me my dad
did not need me there to take care of him.
"You're eleven years old."
And when I persisted, she stole the last vestiges
of my innocence.
"He's got a girlfriend. He doesn't need you. He's leaving us because he
wants his girlfriend more than his wife and kids."

I was depressed before that.

When we moved away to the country,
surrounded by woods and plowed fields.
And I was ten years old
trying to figure out why I felt as empty as an overturned cup.

But I was depressed before that.

Back when—for no reason I could understand—I cried in church
and got shamed for trying to get
attention
I did not deserve.

I tell my therapist that story, even though I know…

I was depressed before that.

Attention

I'm crying. Again.
They are singing words about Jesus loving us
and I am sitting in a hard folding chair
with tears
streaming down my face.
I can't make it stop.
But in this room full
of child voices
lifted in joy,
I am comfortable with my tears.
They feel right.
They feel honest.

A friend in my Sunday School class grabs my hand.
I am warm, like a blanket has been tucked
up under my chin.
A different friend
moves to the empty seat on the other side of me.
She wraps an arm
around my shoulders.
And I feel comfortable,
like I'm listening to a story I've heard twenty times before,
and I know the ending.

The tears are a warning.
They are a beacon,
a lighthouse shining out
over dark and treacherous waters.
I wear them like a badge of courage.

These tears
are my Purple Heart
for surviving
what should have killed me.

A Sunday School teacher
in her self-important
tweed dress ushers my friends
away. They obey,
because we were all taught
in this very room
to obey.
The tweed sits next
to me.
Much too close.
She wraps an arm
around me.
Not warm.
Not comfortable.

She holds me
too tightly.
Like the blanket is smothering me.
Like a villain I never met
just entered my favorite, comfortable story.

"You need to stop this," she chides.
"You're ruining everyone's chance
to feel the spirit.
You're just doing this
for attention.
You're being selfish."
Her arm around me
is too tight. Her hand on my hands in my lap
is a familiar cage.
"You wanted attention. Well, now you've got it."

I can't shrug her off. No matter how hard I try.
She tells me lies
and I begin to believe them.

"Ten-year-olds should be able
to control
themselves better than this," her hiss
fills my ears with the shame
she is trying so hard to impart.
She shakes me a little,
as if intending
to jar me
out of my tears.

It already worked.
They dried
themselves up
and ran away.

Jesus loves everyone.
Except me.

"Church is supposed to be a joyful place."

Joy is the very
        last
            thing
                church has been to me.

But that
is a selfish thought.
A rebellious thought.
A thought I know
I am going to pay for.
Somehow.
Later.
When they stop singing
and the men come
to pull me out of class.
Again.

Whores cry.

 **Now**

Movie

I know I'm not going to like this movie.
My brother picked it.
My dad was excited to see it.
They pressured me into coming.

But I always want to be with my own family.

So I agreed. And now
I am sitting in the center seat,
with my brother beside me,
            and then his wife,
                    and then my stepmother,
                            and then my father on the aisle.

I haven't removed my jacket. I wear it like armor.
Maybe it can protect me from the movie.
Every preview
looks like something
I would never watch.
Slasher or horror that makes me feel
physically sick
and I look into the tub of popcorn
my brother shoves in my lap.

I wish I could just take a nap.

But the movie unfolds.
A story I am wary
of right away.
It's all gray.
Or I remember it that way.
A girl is shot. And then
something
is happening on screen
that makes me need to scream.

I feel a tunnel
  closing in
    around me.
      I am thrust into the dark.

And on screen
a girl is raped on the ground.
And I am trying to figure out
why I am her
and she is me.

I'm a child now,
even though I know I'm a grown woman.

I am a tiny child weeping.

I can hear my child voice
in my own mind
where usually I'm grown.

I sink
as far into the movie seat
as I can.

My brother whispers,
  but I don't know if it's threats
    or attempts at comfort.

You're being selfish.

A child's voice begs,
Please don't hurt me!

And I have to
get away.
Popcorn spills,
the smell makes me ill.

I am climbing over legs
and pushing past my brother,
           his wife,
               stepmother,
                  then my dad.

I am weeping freely and running away.
Even though
I can't get away
from the child in my head who is weeping
and pleading
for the bad stuff
to stop.

I can see the girl on screen
—an actor—
but I am her and she is me.
And we are both the child weeping in my head.

"I know," a woman in the hall tells me kindly. "It's horrible."
She left, too, perhaps, when the unexpected—but completely
forewarned—event unfolded on screen.

There's nowhere to escape to. So I go
to the wall.
I am not as small
as the child still sobbing in my brain.
I can almost hear her name.

"Rachel?" I whisper.
As if someone inside me
could be different than the me
crying openly against the wall
in a public hall.

I am found. Wrapped up
in strong arms.
"What's wrong?"

"Something happened," I tell him in shock. "Something happened to me when I was a little girl."

Yes! Rachel rejoices.
But I'm not hearing voices.
They're in my head.

Something happened.

Dark

I am Rachel
sitting in the dark.

The cabinet surrounds me.
Have I been here for five minutes?
An hour?
Five dark and empty days?

It's hard to say. There is no time in here, in the dark.

On the outside of the cabinet, I hear muffled voices.
Priesthood conversations.
Sometimes near and sometimes far.
I hear the swish of robes
and the smell of revelry.
But I do not get
any blessings
today. Because I cried
and now I'm a whore in the dark.

I tremble
because I know this is not how my punishment ends.
Whores don't deserve respect.
They don't get white veils and soft words, "You're a princess."
Whores get mess.

The cabinet opens, and I know what's coming.
Another whore gets pushed in beside me.
She is still crying.
I don't know her name.
Or maybe I do somewhere,
like at school or church.
But not here.
Not in the Temple of the Holy Josephic Priesthood.

No one here exists outside.
All names and faces
are washed away
in the anointing.
This place is the most sacred in the world.
So I don't know the girl.
But I know that, like me, she's a whore who did not do what she was told.

"Are you ready to be pure?" the High Priest asks me.
The whore he shoves beside me has a gag
over her mouth,
a wisp of cloth
to muffle
her ongoing cries.

But I can't worry about her.
I can only worry about God
and what He wants from me.
I can only worry about purity.

"Yes," I beg. "I'll do anything."

He has a shoestring.
He leans forward
and ties up the hands of the whore.
I shudder when my brain
tries to figure out
what she could have done
to displease God so thoroughly.

"Are you ready to be pure?" he asks me again,
dark eyes shining with what looks like
joy.
But his voice is stern
so I must not know what joy looks like.

I say, "Yes. I want to be pure."
I don't want to be like her.

He points at the girl beside me.
"You can be pure if you do to her—everything I tell you."

I knew that was coming.
I'd been here before.
I'd earned my purity
in this cabinet
in the past.
And I remember, somehow—
though it doesn't last—
that I have been her, too.
Tied and waiting
to be abused
by a child my own age.

 Now

The Shelf

"I don't understand!" I say in a heated voice.
"If something happened to me when I was a little girl,
why don't I remember?"

There's an ember
of something in my therapist's eye.
Compassion, maybe,
but also a deep *knowing* that I cannot identify.

She says, "Sometimes the brain protects itself."

Inside of me there's a shelf.
It has been stacked with so many things
        that the weight
            has started to bear it down.
                Now the shelf is bowed,
                    but I bolster it up in the center
with comfortable lies.

"I probably just made it up."
My brain finishes the thought that I don't say aloud.
For attention.

"Can we try something?" my therapist asks.
She leans forward as if to invite me in.
"Can we try imagining that you didn't make anything up?"

"But, I…"

"For a little while," she presses gently.
Her eyes smile. "Let's allow this situation to exist.
Even if you made it up.
What is it telling you?
If you listen to it."

I humor her. I let myself
pretend it's real—even though it's probably not.
It's worth a shot.

And flickers cross my mind.
- Pencils that make me ill. A dirty joke someone told me in elementary
  school that never left me.
- A toy from infancy that's supposed to bring me joy but fills me with
  dread.
- A muffling cloth.
- A white veil.
- A candle dripping wax.
- A monotone, "By the power of the Holy Josephic Priesthood—which
  I hold…"

Not that! A voice shrieks.

I run away from the door in my mind.

"I think I made it all up," I say and let the door stay shut.

But a whisper of a voice asks again,
Are we okay?

Then   Blessed

"By the authority of the
Holy Josephic Priesthood
—which I hold—
I anoint you,
faithful daughter,
as a Virgin of the Lord."

I am not allowed to wiggle. I must sit completely still.
They have tied me to the Covenant Chair.
God doesn't like wiggles.
He likes silent, still, sweet daughters.

"We anoint your head with the crown of God."
A swipe of oil on the top of my head.
It's a smell that fills my nostrils
with hope and terror.
"May your mind stay focused on your duties as a Virgin of the Lord."

I need to move but I don't.
I stay very, very still.

The oil is pressed against my lips.
A finger slips into my mouth.
I cannot choke on it, even though
it pushes all the way back,
trying to choke me.

"We anoint your tongue
as an instrument
of the will of God
through the Priesthood."

I want to ask them why
the oil has to taste so bad.
But I can't.

I cannot speak or move
at all
during my blessing.
And asking questions of the Priesthood
is a sin.

The oil is pressed against my bare chest.
"We anoint your breast as an instrument
of the will of God through
the Priesthood."

I squeeze my eyes shut.
The worst part is coming.
The part that makes me
squirm sometimes.
But God's blessing
is only given
if the Virgin is completely
submissive.
That means I cannot move a muscle.

The oil swipes across the soles
of both feet.
I squeeze myself tight
and manage not to move
even though it tickles in the worst possible way.

"We anoint your feet
as an instrument of the will of God through the Priesthood."

It's getting closer now.
I know it's coming.
The worst part.

A hand slides down
between my legs and strokes

God's Garden—a place
on my body I am not allowed to touch
without permission. A place
that no one but the Priesthood is allowed
to see, touch, or use.
The oil coats the garden
and then—I squeeze my eyes shut and stay completely still—inside
the garden with a painful, single thrust.

"We anoint your sex as an instrument of the will of God through
the Priesthood."

The next part
is the worst part.
Even worse
than the Garden.
I clench my hands on the Covenant Chair and promise
myself that this time I will stay
completely still. I will not move
and make them start
all over again.

The oily hand slides down my back
and touches the Holy Place
between my bottom cheeks.

And for a moment, I am far, far away.
I am floating above all of this.
I am flying into the darkness   .
where I am not tied to a chair
receiving the Blessing of God.
I am not aware of the hand
on my bottom—the finger in my bottom—and the words
of the Priests
touching me in all
my most
Sacred Places.

"We anoint your base as an instrument of the will of God through the
Priesthood."

> I slam back into the chair
> —even though I never moved a muscle—
> and make myself be still
>> as they finish the
>> Naming and Assignment.

> Now, though, I am angry
> because I never wanted to be here in the first place.
> And I am mad
> that I don't have a choice in the matter.

> "Daughter Beth,
> having been commissioned
> of Jesus Christ,
> I anoint you as a Virgin of the Lord,
> bound through his Priesthood to be a Bride
> for the Holiest of Men.
> Honored child, you are one of God's
> dearest treasures. We give you tonight
> a blessing
> of sweetness and submission.
> We bless you with the sacred secrecy
> of the Highest Priesthood of God.
> Your tongue shall not be able to speak of these things,
> lest it be plucked out.
> And you damned in the pain and torture of Hell.
> Your mind shall not be able to recall these things, lest it
> crumble into darkness.
> And you damned in the pain and torture of Hell.

> We bless you with the will
> to serve the Priesthood
> with all your heart,
>> mind,
>>> body,
>>>> and anointed spaces.

Your stillness
is a submission
to the will of God
and your husband..."

They say his name.
I don't
even listen.
It doesn't matter
what he's called.
He'll be a savage, like the rest of them.
I don't care if they blessed me
with sweetness. In my heart
I want them to be attacked by a pack of wild dogs.

"In the name of the Father, the Son, and the Holy Spirit.
Amen."

Now

Are We Okay?

I am too many.
    I am also too much.
    And not nearly enough.

There are pieces of me that whisper secrets in the dark.
I cry tears that seem to have no source.

 Can I divorce myself? Of course
not.

I am forever stuck with me.

 "Are we okay?" the words torment me with their unrelenting curiosity.
"I'm not okay!" I shout back. And no one hears me,
because I am sitting in a parking lot, in my car,
shouting at myself inside my head.
"I won't go in. Not again!"
My hands clench on the wheel.
My knuckles are white as I fight
with myself.

But the tumult subsides. I sigh
and drag myself out of the car
where I hide.
Because I cannot ever truly hide
from myself.

Are we okay? those words again.
And I am forced
to pause,
my hand hovering above the handle
to the therapy office door.

They are the very same words I heard
over and over before.

Why have I never wondered
at the plural?

 Then

Silent

I am ten years old.
I am in a tiny room
with no windows.
I am pissed, because they don't have a right to me now,
in the daylight.
I know it's daytime
even if there are no windows to prove it.

These men in their suits. They don't know
that I know the truth.
They are animals.

"God resides in the darkness.
He is the light," one of them reminds me.
And he flips the switch
to plunge us into the dark.
But I know I will not find
God here.

The door locks from the inside.

"I don't want to," I try to say,
but I am silenced.
I am always silenced.

"Wants are worldly," says one voice in the dark. "Needs are godly."

I've heard it all before.

"Be a good girl."

And the priests don't anoint me.
For some reason, they don't do that in the daylight.
They don't give me the blessing.
They don't pray over me.

They go straight to what happens
after the Naming and Assignment.

Once, I was blinded by it. But now I'm not.
Their needs are more important than my wants.

My mouth—though not anointed for their use—is filled with them.
My Garden—though not assigned to them—is used by them.
And when I protest or cry,
they choke me.
They remind me, *"Be a good girl."*

Good means silent.

Now   Alyss

Silence is done.

No! I have had enough.
I am not too much.
I deserve to see the light of day.
A part of me has had her way for far too long.
The quiet, weaker part.
And I am strong.
        Strong enough to pull her down and push her out of the way.

She was in the middle of an explanation
that makes no sense.
Another time she tries to explain away my existence.
She tries to flex
her imagination
and say that she made things up
she could never have known.
She is grown into the person I hate most:
one who lies constantly to herself.

And I am done now.
I am done waiting for her to figure it out.
I am done waiting for more patient parts to wear her down with their
constant questions.
I have played by their rules—mostly.
I did not seek attention
even when it cost me.
                Until the cost
                was too high.
        I acted out.
        I bought things that she could not remember buying.
        I made friends under a different name.
        I dated.
        I raided her life in every place I could
until I was caught and shoved back into the dark.

But I am done with the dark.

I am done waiting
and watching her dismiss me
as imaginary.
I am done waiting for her to figure it out for herself.
I am done waiting for this therapist
to finally speak up
and say what we both know is true.

"No!" I say, and from the outside, it looks like I interrupt myself.
But the therapist across from me is not surprised.
Or she's good at hiding it.

"Hello?" she says, and that's my opening.
Because she knows. *I knew it.*

"I'm not Nichole," I tell her firmly.
Nichole is a coward who hides from herself.

She nods and once again says, "Hello.
Can you tell me who you are?"

We've been in therapy with her
for over a year.
I thought she might balk at my appearance.
But she doesn't disappoint.
I knew she was smarter
than Nichole gave her credit for.

"I am *not* Nichole.

Even though I am swathed in her body
and I look out through her eyes,
I have never, ever been Nichole.
She was too weak for what I went through.
I had to be there
for the hard stuff.

43

And she got to live her cozy life
without any of the rough, despicable darkness.
She's a mess.
But she could never guess
what I would say next.

"I am Alyss."

Somewhere deep inside,
Nichole is screaming in denial.
Again.

Then

Bare Feet

I am twelve.
The bike is solid beneath me, the pedals rough against my bare feet.
I'm a country girl now, so my feet are always bare.
But I don't usually ride. I stayed inside
when my brothers and sisters all went to the creek.
I wanted my mom to myself.
We made pink popcorn balls
and laughed together.
It was an afternoon
completely free
of any others.
It was just me
and the woman I want to become.

The bike starts to wobble
as we pedal down the road.
It's not much of a downhill slope. But enough
for me to regret not wearing shoes.
If my shoes even fit me anymore.
I don't like to tell mom when I need more.
She barely has enough money to buy herself a soda.
She needs that more that I want shoes.
We are country kids who go barefoot.

"Mom," I call out in panic.
She rides ahead of me
but looks back at my alarm.

I try to brake
but find my brothers have been tinkering with the bike.
The brakes are gone.
They do this sometimes—take things apart
and put them back together later.
I guess they never got to later.

I'm getting carried away as the bike sways
dangerously side to side,
speeding up so much I cannot control it.

"Mom!"

"Put your feet down!" she cries.

I am a barefoot country kid.
"I can't," I panic.

We were supposed to deliver pink popcorn balls
to my grandmother.
My mom wants to be her when she grows up.

The speed won't let up.
"Mom!" I scream,
but she can't help me.
And an angry, deep part of me says, *She never could.*

And I am floating free in the dark.
Though a moment ago it was afternoon
and I was riding down the rough road with my mom,
now I am somewhere else.
I am alone.
The darkness surrounds me.

>   I am also Alyss
>   and I am hissing at the bike
>   as it sways side to side.
>   I can't put my feet down because—for some stupid
>   reason—I'm not wearing shoes.
>   And the handlebar sways
>   into the pavement.
>   I am tangled in the wreckage.
>   I am mangled
>   by the road.
>   Like everyone, it treats me roughly.

All I see is red.
The blood on my face and hands.
Gravel in places
it should never land.
I am ugly now.
I am sure I will
always be ugly.
And for some reason, that brings me
                              satisfaction.

Silent

She gives me the satisfaction of believing me. Finally.

"How long have you been around?" the therapist asks.
She tried asking about my "birth" but it just confused me.
This is a better question. At least this one is one I can answer.

"Since the bike accident."

At least, that's as far back
as I can remember.
Everything before it feels like darkness.

"Do you want to tell me about it?"

No. But I do.
I lean back against the couch, spread out,
take up space.
And I spit it all out,
"I was afraid to tell my mom I needed shoes.
So, when she told me, 'You should probably put on shoes,' I laughed it off.
It was better than ruining the afternoon I had spent alone with her."
Her neediest child.
I shake off that gloom.
"I rode without shoes
plenty of times.
But the circumstances combined
to make this day a nightmare.
My brothers took the bikes apart to build a go-kart.
They had not finished
putting them back together.
They did not touch my mother's bike, of course.
And I didn't notice they had
tampered with mine."

That was true. Though it was all hazy.
Because that was Nichole.
She abandoned me right before the shitstorm.
I got bam, slam, splatter.
She got darkness and peace.

"I lost control of the bike on a slight hill.
I could not slow down. I could not put my feet down.
I was going too fast and
I had no shoes on.
So when the handlebar hit the road, I was halfway thrown.
My face and hands took the brunt.
I still have scars."

Scars I had been told would
disappear
if I had enough faith.
But faith,
like all things tied to god,
abandoned me.

"I didn't smile for a year."

Probably longer.
My smiles were not joyful.
They were vindictive.
I only smiled when I found a way to upset Nichole.

But *she* did not smile for a year after the accident.
Smiles hurt.

"It's the first thing I remember. Pain and blood," I say.
So it was like a birth in a way.
We are all born through blood and pain, and tears.

"What is your role?" the therapist asks.
I lean back and laugh.

"Blood and Pain."

 Then

Pain and Blood

I am six years old.
There is blood on my white veil.
But I did not cry this time.
I am getting stronger. Like God wants me to.

When they say, "Good girl,"
I bloom.

I have been chosen among all the daughters of the earth
to be a sacred tool
for the Priesthood.
It's an honor so few deserve.
But I do, because I'm being good.

My Husband takes me back to the sacred waiting space.
I'm alone in there.
Only then do I let myself cry.
I wipe and I wipe.
I am trying to fix everything
before they come back
and anoint me again.
For someone else.
But the loneliness
and the cry of other Virgins
in other rooms,
and the candlelit darkness
combine
to make me tremble.
I am not strong enough this time to stay.
"I want to get away," I whisper.
And then I fall into the black,
enveloping sweetness.

But I'm also still in the room.
And now I'm angry.

I won't let them hurt me anymore.
I slip out the door.

I am caught by
an Angel at the exit.
We call them Angels because
they wear white and don't talk.
They hope to one day become Priests
and earn Virgin wives.

He carries me without saying a word.
He brings me back
to the candlelit world
and tosses me into the office
      at the feet of the Highest Priest.

"What happened?" he demands.

And the Angel speaks. I've never heard their voices before.
"She ran," it breaks from deep to a prepubescent squeak.

The Highest Priest glares at me and says, "Hello, Beth."

He knows it's me.
      It has to be me.
Rachel and the others would never try to run.

"I guess it's time for more fun."

What the High Priest considers fun
makes him a bad, bad man.
I know that.
But he's stronger and more powerful than I am.
He drags me,
screaming,
out of the quiet and candlelit temple rooms.

Into the musty room with the bad.
With the terrifying.

"I'm sorry! I'm so sorry!" I scream.
But he doesn't care.
He knows
I'm not really sorry.
He knows I'm only scared of what he'll do to me.

I have reason to be scared.

He opens a lid on a trashcan.
"Whores are better off drowned," he tells me.
And then he plunges me in.

Fight as I do,
I can never win.

And the can is full of moldy-smelling water.
I am doused
and held down.
I know this time he will kill me for not being a faithful
daughter.
I cry for my father.
For my mother.
But only in my mind.
My mouth is too full of water and terror to cry.

He pulls me up by my hair
long enough to get a breath of stale air.
Then down I go again.
I'm going to drown
this time,
and my parents will never know
where I went.
They will be confused.
If they notice I'm gone.

He yanks me back out again. "Is Beth gone?"
I'm still here but admitting it is death.
"Yes," I lie.
Lies are also death.
"Yes. I'm Rachel."

"Rachel is a daughter of God!"
he is not fooled.
"Beth is a whore."
He pushes me down once more.
Daughters of God,
Virgins of the Lord,
quiet and obedient girls
are not nearly killed.
Only the whores.
Only the ones who fight and try to get away.

"What did I say?" he demands when I reemerge,
spluttering and sobbing and drooling all over his black
robes.
"What did I say last time?"

I know the answer.
It's the same every time.
Every time I try to get away
or resist the will of God.

"It's better to be dead than disobedient," I cry.
And I know it's a lie.
Everything they say is a lie.

Except one thing:
"I will kill you to save God's Work."
He means he will kill me if I tell.
And I know him well.

He'll do it.

Drowning

"I have D.I.D.," I say on repeat. I can't make the words go any deeper.
They stay trapped
                on the surface of my tongue
and can't penetrate into my brain.
I'm a trainwreck.

"I have D.I.D."

My therapist has seen me when
I'm not me.
She's talked to me
when I was not there.
Except I was there.
I don't remember.
                Or rather, it's hazy.
Like something that happened in a faraway dream, back in childhood.
It's like déjà vu and hysteria had a baby.

"D.I.D."

It stands for multiples of me.
I am a we.

Are we okay?
Not today.

"Dissociative Identity Disorder," my therapist explains.
But it's like a trumpeted fanfare
from the highest tower.
I have parts that hide from me.

"How? Why?" I ask her in desperation.

It's the divorce.
It's the heartbreak.
It's my dad's abandonment.
It's the affair.
It's my best friend telling me to be careful not to follow my parents to hell.
It's my dad's "best" that's really the bare minimum.
It's my brothers who never lifted a finger.
It's bread, made from scratch, with a wheat-grinder, twice a week.
It's prairie dresses and no friends.
It's my mother never getting out of bed.
It's daily breakfasts before Scripture study, when my mother is off with a hidden boyfriend.
It's kids who need me to be their parent when I'm their sister.
It's the never-ending ritual of lies from the pulpit.

I can't find a single culprit.

"D.I.D. is usually the result
of repeated
and severe
trauma."

I shake my head. "But that's not what happened to me."

She nods and says, "Usually."

But there is something in her eyes
that tells me she doesn't believe me.
But what she's saying is
I can't believe myself.

That's the end of my shelf.
                          It crumbles
                and all the "that doesn't
          make sense"
      comes tumbling down.
And I am drowned in it.

I can't keep my head above water.

"I was a good Daughter."
But the tears on my face tell another story.
My mother should sing my praises:
because I was everything she never deserved.
My father should pause and consider:
I was *perfect* because otherwise I knew I'd lose him.

But deep in my bones,
I know I'm not
a faithful daughter.
Somehow,
I am a filthy whore.

Then Beth

They named me Beth.
I'll never forgive them
for giving me a name and a blessing.
Not the same one I got at the tiny age of newborn,
held in the hands of ignorant assholes
who don't know how precious is the bundle they hold.
And they proclaim I belong to god.
And give me a name.
And I am a baby, swaddled in a white, uncomfortable dress.
And I can't complain
because I'm not able to speak yet.
But they name me and give me to a church
                                    that has a seedy underbelly.
The name they gave me then was Nichole.

But now I'm Beth.

In the dark
I was renamed.
Again and again.
When they named me Beth
it was so someone would know
how dangerous it is to displease the Lord.
I was named to be a Whore.

I was anointed but I spurned their advances.
The Highest Priest knew Rachel would never disobey.
Evelyn was always quiet and respectful.
Sadie was a good girl.

Beth was made to pay.

They tied me up. Just a wrap around my mouth
and a cloth around my wrists.

And my panties pulled up too high,
too tight.
He wanted me uncomfortable.
And he shoved me
into a room
that smelled like paint.

It was a place
I had never been before.
They had been asking for me
more and more.
I'd been in rooms I did not want to remember.
I had been manhandled by men who wanted a challenge.
I was bound
        and smacked
                and drowned.

I was buried up to my neck in cement.
And they said they would let me dry in it.
But they didn't.
They pulled me out,
scraped and weeping.
And I was pleased enough to thank them.
To cooperate.
To be relieved at my escape.
My skin still hurts from that.
It was not long enough ago for me
to have forgotten.
I tried to be
good
afterward.
But that's not what he wants now.
He likes
to make me suffer.

This room is new to me.
It has a dollhouse
on a table
in the center of the room.

I can't help but bloom.
I told the High Priest once
that all I wanted
was a dollhouse.

"Is this for me?" my eyes ask.
I cannot speak around the gag.
But even this question
makes me afraid it's a sin to ask anything of the Priesthood.
A sin I'll be slapped for.

But his eyes glitter and he smiles.
"Look closer."

I do.
I get closer,
and he shines a light on it.
And it's not just a dollhouse.
It's *my* house.
It is a tiny,
perfect representation.
I am blown away.
He spins it
and shows me the rooms inside.
There are dolls made of cloth and wire.
My family.
There's Daddy in the living room watching TV.
And there's Mommy in the kitchen.
I see dolls of my brothers.
My baby sister is in her playpen.
But I don't see me.

When I look back at the Highest Priest,
he's holding the doll
that's supposed to be me.

"Do you want to be there?" he asks
and moves it closer to the house.

I always want to be with my own family.

I do.
I desperately do
want to be there,
away from the Highest Priest
and this nightmare. But I don't
know what answer he wants.
I'm too wary.
I shake my head slightly.

It's both no and it's yes.

He laughs again. A laugh I know then I will never forget.

"Guess what?"

We are not alone in the room.
Suddenly a couple fires bloom
in front of the faces of other Priests.
I thought they were busy with other Virgins,
doing their godly duty.
But no.
They are here for me,
with lighters lit in front of their glittering black eyes.

He puts the doll that is me on the table
beside
the house.
Not in the house.
Not close enough.

"I'm going to show you what will happen if your mouth decides to be a
whore."

Whores cry.
They scream.
They talk.

Good girls are silent.

The other men move forward
and they light my house on fire.
It's new. I smell fresh paint.
It's a beautiful, new dollhouse.

"It's all your fault," the men whisper. "It's all your fault."

My mind yells, *Lies.*
But then I watch the tiny house catch fire.
They are burning it.
My whole family is inside.
And they are burning my house down.

And maybe because
I am only a little girl
with a big imagination,
or maybe because they hoped
I would see it,

I am standing on the sidewalk in front of my house watching it burn down.
"God punishes whores."

I know it's true.
The house burns and I'm not allowed to look away.
My family is burned
while the tiny me and the real me
watch it happen.

And I'm not sure if it's only a dollhouse,
or if it's my real house.
I don't know if it's a threat
or a boast of what they've done.
I don't know if my tiny baby sister is now gone.

I only know one thing:
God is more powerful than whores like Beth.

Invisible

I am Evelyn. And I am four years old.
But I am also fully grown and living in a grownup body.
It's a silly way to live.

But I get to be both an adult and a kid
because of D.I.D.
It's a blessing and a mystery.

It saved our life.
It saved our sanity.

And now I'm a little girl playing with ponies but still able to reach the high
shelf.

And it's daytime.
That's scary but also neat.
I've played in the dark in secret for many, many years. Now I'm here
and I feel free.
But still scared to be me.

What if someone sees? My job is to be invisible.

Nichole is afraid of me.
Afraid of *me*.
A little girl whose job was always to be sweet.
I'm not scary.
I'm a secret that I keep.

But when Nichole finds toys of mine,
she gets panicky.
Because she wants to be normal.
She wants to blend in.
She wants to be invisible.

And toys mean we're not invisible.

But I want to play
and I get to.
Because we are not hiding
anymore.

We are talking to the nice lady in the quiet office.
We are eating pancakes with the nice lady in my house.
We are talking to each other finally.
No more *Shh! Shh! Shh!* for me.

I get to be visible now.
But I still put the toys away when I'm done.

Rabid Dogs

I am eleven years old.
My cousin and I are walking
down a road
we've walked before. Every year.
After the turkey is put away
and the leftovers are stacked in the fridge,
I like to walk.

There's something about this holiday
that doesn't
feel
right. It doesn't feel
good.
It feels like
screaming
in my mind. So I walk.
We walk.

But the neighbor's dogs have another idea this year.
They approach, snarling. A pack of them.
Dozens.
Maybe hundreds.
I don't stay to count them.

I turn away. Back
to the house
and another kind of wild dogs.
If they come for me again. They haven't since I moved here.

My cousin runs ahead,
screaming. But I walk
slowly.
I know this scene. It's familiar
in some uncomfortable way.

If I run, the dogs will follow me up into the yard, to the little kids. I'll
endanger them.
So I move
slowly.
Don't spook the dogs.
And when I feel one nip my thigh,
I sigh.
This feels familiar.
But familiar is not always *right*.

Neediest

"I am my mother's neediest child."
My therapist seems unsurprised.
She must know that I'm needy like an ungrateful houseplant,
sitting in the sun
making demands
for water and nutritious soil.
Doing nothing
except sitting there.
Not earning my keep.

"Is it wrong to have needs?"
Her question is meant
to break me
into
      a million
              tiny
                    pieces.
Like a plant crumbling from lack of water.

"I can't be needy."
The words feel vulnerable.
And true.
Maybe the truest words I've ever said to her.

"Why?"

 What kind of question is this? Why is she trying to trap me? Does she
know I'm steeped in guilt for all my endless needs?

"Because…"
I have no answer to her question. But someone else does.

I can feel them pushing.
Pushing.

I let go
        and
             fall
                  away.

And I am Beth now.
Except I don't go by Beth anymore.
I named myself and gave myself
my own blessing.
One that Priests would neither accept
nor allow.
But I won't bow to them again.
"Because if I have needs, then they can be exploited."
It's a big word and a bigger concept.

"Where did you learn that?" the therapist asks.

I don't answer out loud. But in my mind, I whisper,
In the Dark.

 Then

Invisible

In the dark, I weep.

"What do you need?" asks a kindly voice.
He strokes my hair as tears
—those tiny cold betrayals—
slide down my cheeks.

I am hurt.

I am broken.

This time, they broke me, and my tears slipped out.

"Time," I whisper. Or something like that. Maybe, "I need a break."
Or perhaps, "I need a minute."
I'm not sure what I say. Something like
"Please let me have a moment to compose myself."

But his smile is dark and I know he will deny me.

"No. Right now is not about you. Submit to the Priesthood."

I beg as he forces me back to the bed, back to my back,
backwards
where he expects me to accept his will,
"Please!"

"Submit!" he insists.

And I am drowning in my needs. They have betrayed me.

Obscured Passages

I am weeping in a quiet, comforting place.
A bridge over a river greets me—a sedate hanging on the wall.
I fall over the bridge and drown in my trauma.
Clutch the end of the couch
And tap, tap, tap until my hand goes still.

My therapist lets me cry.
She always
lets
me
cry
without judgment.
Without expectations.

I am allowed to be the broken toddler.
The neglected child.
The thunderstruck preteen.
The too grownup teenager.
The confused young woman.
The heartbroken woman.
The shattered human with too many parts,
        too many pains, too many memories of torture and strain.

She allows me to be all the parts of me.
So I cry. Because a girl has needs.

A toddler and a child and a preteen have needs.
A woman has needs.
They all need to cry
for their devastating childhood lost to the Holy Josephic Priesthood.

We cry together—an act of unification.
And for a few moments, we are all one.
But only for a few moments.

Because a shattered mind does not
come back easily or quickly
from obscured passages,
     darkened corridors,
          bramble-tortured pathways of the brain.

But weeping together helps us find our way to each other.
I stare at the bridge over a river on the wall.
I let the tears fall.
They create a river
on which we all float to a central location.
I am surrounded by the voices,
and in my mind they now have faces.
They are all
me
and somehow
not me.

Replaced

Somehow, I'm returned to my bed.
Hours in the dark do not prepare
me for morning around the corner.
I can't imagine how I will be a girl in the regular world again.
Because I'm a Whore of the Earth.

Every move I make
displeases god.
I don't know him, but I know we won't get along.
He uses his power to punish.
To torture.
To label me a word that means
I won't knuckle under.
A word that means I fight when I should submit.
A word that means I displease him.
Because my purpose is to displease him.
To fight the Priesthood.

But my anger recedes
                as I fade backward.

And a Good Girl replaces me.
A Good Girl who says her prayers
and reveres god
and respects the Priesthood.
She has a different name and a different purpose.
She is angelic,
like the Priesthood wants.
Like god wants.
She would get along with god
because she never breaks the Laws.
She is a beautiful, naive blur of submission.

She lays her head on a lumpy pillow
and closes her eyes.

Tiny lashes against soft cheeks.

Because morning is coming
and the world outside the dark spaces
will expect to see

a joyful, well-rested child.

And I am in the dark

with my pain and rage.

Now

To Be

"I have D.I.D.," I say aloud to my best friend.
She smiles a knowing smile.

"Yes," she agrees. Because she knows what she has seen.
She knows that she's always known many parts of me.
Now, she has relationships with other parts.
        She has dreams of them.
She has entire conversations with them
that I do not remember.
They are me but they are not me
        exactly.

"I don't know how to be this person," I declare.
I wipe my eyes,
hurry away tears that have no right
to interrupt me.

She smiles. "Just be."

As if that is the easiest answer in the world.
        But
I don't know how to be.
                That's the problem.
                        It's the solution to another's problem.

I can never just be,
        because I was made
                to not be.

 Then   Happy

"God made little girls to be happy."
I hear those words again.
They are a prayer.
They are a promise.
They are a curse.

But I make my smile
and nod my head.
I look down like I know I should.
Don't look the Priesthood in the eyes.

A stinging pain and a shock
through my body
are the first hints that
he slapped me.
The Priesthood.

It's a test I have failed before.
When I look up instead of keeping my eyes on the floor.

"Answer me!" he orders.
"Yes, sir."
"Are you happy?" he thunders.
He is not happy.
But God did not make the Priesthood to be happy.

I nod my head vigorously.
I smile even though there are tears
sliding down my cheeks.
Heavy like my heart is.
Eager to escape the man
who slaps my face again.
Testing me to see if I can be what God made me to be.

I grin. I will show him how happy I am.
"Yes, sir. I am happy."

It feels like a lie.

But he grasps my face and says, "That's right.
Because you have no reason to be unhappy
as long as you obey the Priesthood."

He forces me to see his cold, dark eyes.
Then his mouth presses against my forehead

as praise
for being what he wants.

Another dark robe.
Another Priesthood in the doorway.
"She won't cry on me?" he asks in a voice
that sounds like he doubts me.

The Priesthood strokes my smiling face
and wipes away my tears.
"Not Lily," he tells the other one.
"Lily knows her place."

A rustle of paper. A tiny envelope
from one Priesthood to another.
And, like that packet,
I change hands.

The new one picks me up and tosses me
onto his shoulder.
I am staring downward, toward the floor.
But I arch to take one last look at the Priesthood
with that envelope in his hand.
I think he will be looking at me.
He will be reminding me with his eyes that I am a good girl.

But he's looking at the envelope.

I have to tell myself
I am a good girl.

"We're running low on time,"
rumbles the voice of the robe beneath me.
"Are we going to bless her? Or can I just go on?"
He sounds mad. Like I did something wrong.

"I already blessed her," the Priesthood lies.
His eyes
lift from the envelope
to look past me.
Beyond me and my red face.
I don't exist to him now.
"And named her Lily. She's ready."

I don't feel ready.
I feel scared.
I feel a part of me screaming
deep inside.
Warning me.
Telling me to run.
Not that I can, with my feet dangling
uselessly
above me.
I am carried away.

The last thing I see is the Priesthood
put the envelope
in a black
      metal
         box.
And he smiles.

It reminds me,
God made little girls
to be happy.
No matter what.

Headspace

I'm staring at the door in my mind
behind which are the unknown pieces of me.
"I want to go through," I whisper to my therapist.

No! is a stern response in my own mind.

But my therapist is not so decided
against the idea.

"Can we talk about your brain?"
It's a question she asked me before.
Months and months ago,
when she had me paint a picture of my brain.
She was trying to diagnose me then
with what she knew must be a deeper explanation
for my behavior.
For my depression.
For my trauma.

And I painted a library.

"Okay," I reply, unsure if she's
changing the subject or not.
Because in my mind, in my heart,
I'm still standing on the outside of that door.
Always on the outside.

"Some people with Dissociative Identity Disorder
have spaces in their minds for alters to see each other.
Spend time together.
Communicate."

I know this. I've heard of it.
Read about it in my forays
into the wild and untamed world
of the internet.

And it sounded like people who wanted to tell
elaborate stories
to themselves
                    and should take up writing as a hobby.

"A headspace," I reply, knowingly.
And she gives me the scowl that I know
means she has noted that I'm not following her instructions:
do not research my disorder.
"An inner world."

Her playful scowl gives way to a smile.
"I'm wondering if you
have a space like that."

"No," I say out loud,
contemptuous.

Yes, a voice in my head replies.
Contemptuous.
Derisive over my lack
of knowledge
about myself.

I try for bold but my internal question
comes out as timid, *We have a space like that?*

His snort of derision
makes me flinch.
But he answers my question.
Yes! It's the library.
You painted a picture of it, idiot.
That's the place where we can go
to see each other. If any of us
even wanted to do that.
His scoff makes it clear
that he does not have any reason to go there.

Thank you, I tell him.
He scoffs at me again.
But I ignore it.
I answer my therapist,
"Collum tells me that there is a place. The library."

School Library

I'm sitting in the library on the floor.
My teacher has already taken our class away.
I'm supposed to be in line
with them, carrying a book or two back to class
so it will get lost in my desk
for a week
until the next time I come here.

I don't move or make a sound.
I sit in a corner, surrounded
by the smell and safety of books.
I'm in the Dr. Seuss section.
His silly worlds
are often my refuge.
They are impossible.
And they fill me with hope.

Imagination is always where I go to be free.

"What are you doing?"
The voice makes me feel panicky.

I look up and see the school librarian
giving me a curious look.
But she's not glaring.
She's not angry.
I expected her to be.

"Your class already left, hon,"
she tells me, and squats
to look me in the eye.
I'm afraid to answer with the truth:
I know they're gone.
I know I should be with them.
And I'm hiding.

"Did you find a book you want?"
she looks at the Seuss in my hand.
"You can get a chapter book, too."
Big nine-year-old kids like me are expected
to read chapter books.
Not baby books like Dr. Seuss.
But she doesn't scold me.
"I love *The Sneetches.*
Have you read it?"

She stands up
and pulls it from the shelf.
She places it in my hands.
"Give it a try. You can stay here for a little while longer."

I don't know why she's being so nice to me.
But it makes me cry.
"Thank you!" I breathe out a sigh.
She smiles and nods.
Then she leaves me alone.
And I have never been so grateful.

Now

The Door

"I want to go through the door,"
I tell my therapist
again.

In her office,
I am surrounded by books,
soft colors,
light,
and safety.

In this office, I feel free.

But she can still surprise me,
"Okay."

I grab a pillow from beside me, hug it tightly,
and close my eyes.

I move toward the locked door in my mind.
Uh-uh. Don't go there.
But I ignore the stern warning.
I push the door open
and I am falling
                backward
                        through darkness.

Counting

I run into my friend's house.
I am laughing. We are planning
something silly to do outside
in the daylight hours.
Before the darkness descends.
We are playing pretend.

She leads me up the stairs.

In the kitchen on the counter,
there's a black
          metal
              box.

I stop dead.
I don't
follow my friend
down the hall
to her room.
I am confused
as I look
at the box.

That container
should not be here.
It does not fit here.
I know, somehow,
it belongs somewhere else.
With the Priesthood.

I start counting.
I am counting
the envelopes
beside it.

Tithing slips.
And my brain
is trying
to correct
this error.
It's something
I should never
have seen.
So I count.
      Count.
          Count.

"Nichole?" asks a motherly, kindhearted voice.
My friend's mom walks into the room.
"Are you okay? You're white as a sheet."
So cliché.

Sheets aren't white.
They are black
or crimson red.
Sheets bring dread.

I'm counting
all the exits now.
One, two, three…

I pee on my clothes.
It's a way out
all on its own.

"Nichole? Nichole!"
She shakes my shoulders
but I'm not Nichole.
        I'm Evelyn
        and I don't understand
        why there's daylight
        streaming through windows of this house.
        I look up at the woman,
        over at the tithing box.

And she sees what I've seen.

"Oh dear," she whispers to herself.
She sweeps the tithing envelopes
into an open drawer.
She grasps the black box
and shoves it under the sink.
In the dark.
Where it belongs.
Where I belong.

I'm not supposed to be here
in Nichole's life.
This isn't right.
I was created and anointed
in the dark.
I was made for the Priesthood.
But there's no Priesthood here.
Only a woman with fear
in her eyes.

"I think you need to go home."

I don't know where that is.
I've never been out
in the daylight before.
But my legs are wet down to my socks.
I will get into trouble.
I am in trouble.

I turn and run.
I count
my steps as I run up the street.
One… two… three…

A voice in my brain orders,
Calm down!
No one can know.
It's a voice I know.

A distant, quiet, stern voice that seems adult.
A man.
He tells me to go home.
And somehow I know the way.

Library

Somehow, I know the way.

When I open my eyes,
I am surrounded by books.
The smell is overpowering.
Old books. New books.
They are on shelves all around me,
higher than my head, unorganized.
They are stacked, shelved, heaped, and cluttered.
All around.

I wander.
I see books I recognize.
Jane Austen's name on a gold-foiled cover.
Dr. Seuss.
The Screwtape Letters.
Corrie Ten Boom.
The Giver.
And many volumes of Scripture.
Some with names
I don't recognize right off.
The Book of Brigham
and *The Rites of the Holy Josephic Priesthood.*
That one gives off an aura of danger,
so I move away.

I am in a labyrinth of books.
Shelves give way to more shelves.
Madeline was left on an end table.
She looks happy there, I think.
I am amused at the depth of my imagination.
This is such a brilliant illustration
of my mind.
And I'm inside.

"Nichole?" the voice is surprised.
I turn and find her eyes.
Blue, like mine.
Hair in two pigtails.
She's a little girl.
She's me, I think,
but then she says,
"I'm Evelyn."
My grandmother's name.
I wonder who chose it for her.

"Hi," I say.
I know of her.
She used to cry a lot in my brain,
but she's quieter now.
She's happy and safe.
She's the one who comes out
and plays
with the toys hidden in the back of my closet.
She still feels she has to hide
them because when I used to find
them, I would give them away
and be confused for days
about how they got there in the first place.

"Are you lost?" she asks with a giggle.
"It's easy to get lost."

I realize with a shock,
"I don't know my own mind."

Evelyn offers her hand to me.
"You're safe in the library."
Safe.
It feels like a lie.
Like imagination.
But when I look around me,
I realize
imagination is not a lie.

Nothing is truer than this space
Evelyn and I imagine together.

I take her hand.
"I'll show you," she says with confidence
and the childhood lisp
that I've heard before in the dark.

"You're safe here."
Safe feels unreal.
But I was always safest in the library.

Then   Unobscured

It's unsafe
to smile
at the Highest Priest.
He doesn't
like
when I smile unless
                         it's his idea.
And this time,   it's not.

He slaps me to take the smile away,
but it doesn't work
because he trained us to smile
anyway.

"How dare you look the Priesthood in the eyes!"
It's not a question.
It's an accusation.
I don't answer him.
He doesn't want me to.
But that's not why I don't.
I don't
because the real reason would bring me more punishment
than keeping silent and sweet.
Well…silent, anyway.
Beth was never made for sweetness.

I dared to look
because I know something
I'm not supposed to know:

He exists.

I was created in this darkness.
I was formed by the Priesthood.
For the Priesthood.

OBSCURED PASSAGES

In the absence of Nichole,

I was born
in blood and pain.
I only ever existed in this darkness.

Except for another darkness. The one in my mind.
I exist there, too.
And not alone.
There are others with me.
Sadie being a Good Girl.
Lily smiling no matter what.
Rachel carrying the weight of this place they call a temple.

But in my real temple—the dark one in my mind—I am surrounded by books
and other little humans who were made
to be Brides in the temple
        so Nichole did not have to.
        So Nichole could live her life.

There are others who whisper in the book temple:
Collum who tries to hurt us with his words so words can't hurt him.
Nikki who never smiles ever.
And Girl who never even got a name because she was treated like an animal.
And Evelyn.
Evelyn.
Evelyn.

She whispered something in the book temple.
She told us about being at the front—in the body—living Nichole's life
when suddenly Nichole wasn't there anymore.

        Nichole is not allowed in the Temple of the Josephic
        Priesthood.
        How could she go on being a regular girl
        if she had to do what we do?

She couldn't. So she's not allowed to be there.
She's not allowed
to see anything.
Know anything.
Be anything
except Nichole—a "normal" girl.

Evelyn told us about the cashbox and the tithing envelopes
on the counter in the real world.
She told us about peeing her pants
and escaping to Nichole's house
and living Nichole's life
for a few hours.

And I learned:
We have a power…
We   —who have never had anything except a name and a blessing—
have each other.

But there's more…
I know the truth now about the Highest Priest of the Holy Josephic
Priesthood.
He exists.
He's not just some nightmare trapped down here in this basement
temple.
He is somewhere else sometimes.
Someone's father. Someone's husband. Someone's son.
Someone's bishop.

He was not able to keep me
down here
where he expects me to stay.
Because we have each other.
And Evelyn told us all,
"I think he's our friend's dad."

How very sad
to have a father who uses another's daughter
as his own plaything and property
in the name of god.

Not that I know "our friend,"
Because all I know
is darkness.

He's not done with me.
He can see in my face that he lost something.
Instead of giving me to another black robe,
he decides to keep me for himself.
I'm
his
bride
tonight.

And I will put up a fight,
        because that's what I was made to do.
And he will win.
        Because he's a grownup,
        and they
        are the best cheaters.

But he can never make me unlearn.
He can never
change
what has been
unobscured.

Home

I follow Evelyn,
attached to her tiny hand.
"Where am I?" I ask the girl.

She grins back at me.
"You're safe here."

The shelves surrounding us
give way to a set of doors,
standing open.
Evelyn leads me inside.
There is too much to see
that my mind forces me to focus
on only one thing at a time.

There is the man with the stern voice,
standing at the head of the table in a suit and tie.
"Evelyn! What are you doing?"

She does not seem worried
about the sternness.
"I'm bringing Nichole home."

Home is somewhere inside my head.

"Home?" my voice cracks as I ask it.
"Yep," Evelyn says. "Look!"

I look,
and my mind
lets me see more
than the stern-voiced man.

I see Collum, with his persecutor smile, sitting on top of the table.
I see Sadie watching me with her Good Girl hands folded in her lap.
I see Alyss scowling from where she sits backward in her chair.
They are all there.
I search in concern for Rachel
and find her looking back at me
with an ocean of trauma in her eyes.
And beside her, the Whore that was once Beth.
Her arms are crossed
as she condemns me.
And there are more.
>   More.
>   More.
So many more of them
than I knew.
More than the dozen I promised myself there would be.
There's more to me.

"Home," I say again,
and this time it's not a question.
Home is where I am.

Home is where *I* am.

Then   Move

I'm leaving home.

My mother tells me
        we have to move.

"What?" I'm overwhelmed with the news.

"We are moving out of state."
Three states away.

"I can't. I have to stay."
The words are right
even though
        they don't
        make sense.
I have to stay
because
my mission is here.

But my mother
doesn't understand.
How can she?
I earned my sweetness
through silence.

"I belong here."
It feels like a lie.

I don't belong anywhere.
I am a product of too many worlds.
Of too many passages
in too many woods.
Of too many passages
telling me what I should and shouldn't be.

There is nowhere
that accepts me for all the parts of me.

"You can't stay here,"
my mother tells me with a grin.
"You're only ten."

I'm ten. But I'm also five, six, and four,
and an ageless stern man
behind a closed door.
I am timeless
and trapped
in a ten-year-old body.

If I move away, how will the Priesthood find me?
They are words I don't understand
but they feel important. Dire.

"I can't," I plead.

"You need to understand," she tells me.
"We are moving away to be a family again."

Again? I don't even know
what that means.
I always want to be with my own family.
Isn't that what I believe?
It's obscure.
I can't make it make sense.

"I can't," I tell her again.

She points to her chest.
"I'm unhappy.
You know I've been unhappy.
I need to go be close to my family."

To slavering dogs that chase girls down.
"I need to be in a place where I belong."
Where shoes will become obsolete.
"I need to be away from here."
Where I will become my mother's neediest child.
"I need this."

Her needs
are more important.

I need to be here,
where I was blessed
and anointed.
Where the Priesthood can use me.
Not in the dark
anymore, because I've outgrown
the temple.
But in the daylight,
in church,
when they tear me away
from Sunday School
and take me into a dark room
that locks from the inside.
I am a bride.
Leaving
is my damnation.
But submission was always my mission.

I am too confused
about who I am
to argue. I give in.
"Okay."

She needs to get away.
And she doesn't know
that her needs
will send me to hell.

A voice inside whispers,
This time, her needs might save me.

Family

Evelyn takes a seat in an empty chair.
She waves at me to join her. But I stop and stare
at the people around me. People who
are me, but are not me.
Part of me, but parts
that are themselves as well.

I see myself
scattered
around.

Pieces of me that
were child brides.
And Whores of the Earth.
A piece that was a bike accident victim.
A piece that internalized the pain.
A piece that was my mother's neediest child.
A piece that carried me through college.
One that fought off bullies.
One that is a spray of rainbows and banners.
Another that was forced to prove their purity.
One that grew up in an instant of stolen innocence.
One that did not run from the dogs.
Another that watched a dollhouse burn.
An infant in someone's arms.
And they are all me.
And I am the fattest person in the room. As always.
But every pound
of me is made of them.
I am a hundred
or thirty-two.
I don't know. Because I don't count them.
I don't count me.

"Are we okay?" I ask them all. My internal family.
The stern voice comes, still stern
but with an edge of gentleness, "Yes."
We are okay.

Me and the voices that do not mean
I am crazy.
The voices that are
all me.
They lived pieces of life
I couldn't.
My imagination
was a superpower that gave me distance
from what was—at the very least—a situation
too difficult for a child.

"I'm okay," I say.
And when I open my eyes, I am in the office with my therapist.
And she is looking at me with concerned,
$\qquad$ quiet,
$\qquad\qquad$ respectful,
$\qquad\qquad\qquad$ understanding eyes.

"You're okay," she replies.
It might be a question, or just a confirmation of what I said.

"I have D.I.D.," I whisper.
It's a revelation. It should be a passage of scripture:

> And it came to pass that Nichole had D.I.D.
> For her pains were without number, uncounted
> millions of times her needs were met with scorn
> and trickery. And it came to pass that she was she.
> Every part of her was she. And she them. Verily.

Or some other nonsense.
It feels divine.

"You have D.I.D.," the therapist confirms.

I've spent
the past months
not allowing myself to believe
there was an answer
to the confusion.

"There's no solution."

She smiles at me. "You don't need to be solved."

"I just need to be,"
my best friend's words trickle out of my mouth.
Into my heart.
I spent my life trying to fix me because I thought I was broken.

"I'm in parts."

She nods and promises me, "But you won't always be

in pieces."

Then   The Plane

I've gone to pieces.
Tears brushed hurriedly away,
I'm passed off to a woman
in a tailored tweed suit.
The tweed is kinder than I expect her to be.
"Come with me."
She walks away from the solid ground
onto a jetway.
"Are you excited?"

I'm not. I'm gloomy.
I feel like I'm leaving myself behind.
I'm getting on a plane to fly
to a new house.
A new life.

But I am nothing
if not polite.

"Yes," I lie.
I earned my sweetness
through well-timed fibs.

"Is this your first time flying?"

I lie again,
"Yes."

It's my first flight alone anyway.
That counts.
She promises me I won't be alone.
"I'll be checking on you the whole time."

I smile politely.
But I know the truth.
I have always been alone.

Even on this plane, crowded with people,
I'm alone.
Even in a family with children everywhere you step,
I'm alone.
Even with a church full of people
calling out to God and promising to be faithful,
Even with parents down the hall from my empty bedroom.
I was always, always alone.

I sit in the seat and watch through the windows
as the mountains I've always known recede.
My home.
The place where I was important,
and blessed, and special, and sacred.
The place where I was abused and broken.
It falls away *into the trauma of the past.*

I blink and the whole thing is gone.
And I'm in a plane moving toward an unknown destination.
And I don't know
that this move is saving me.
I don't know
that it's protecting me.
I don't know
that it has already ripped me away
from the hands of men who never, ever deserved me.

I don't know
hat this chapter is closing a door
that will be guarded for nearly three decades
by a stern voice in the recesses of my mind.
Uh-uh. Don't go there.

I am just depressed.
I don't know why.
I feel bereft.
Like something epic is over.
I don't know that it was
epically bad,

because I am a child
who was taught strange ideas
about good and bad.

I'm a child
who doesn't want to move away
from the bizarre and twisted
form of "love" I was offered
in a candlelit temple.

I'm a child who is angry
and being forced to submit *again*
to something I do not want.
Change.

The plane flies me away
to a place where they won't be able to find me.
I'm free.

But the parts of me that belonged to them
go muttering into the darkness.
They hide among dark bookshelves.
In corners.
Maybe with Dr. Suess,
but probably other stories.
>   *All the parts of me*
>   *don't love the same things.*

And I am left staring out a window,
wondering why
I am so melancholy.
Wondering why
a moment before I knew
who I was *and my calling.*

Now I am lost.

We are free, says a voice I almost recognize.

But freedom doesn't feel
comfortable.
I ask him the question I will ask
a thousand times
over the next few decades:
Are we okay?

Yep, he answers. *We are okay.*

Now

I'm a writer. I usually write fiction.
But sometimes my heart calls me
to write truth.

This truth is harder
than the hardest piece of fiction.
It is colder and more damning.

I have Dissociative Identity Disorder
because I was a victim
of severe and repeated
neglect and abuse.
I have come to terms
with that now.
Or part of me has.

The trauma formed around me
and through me
and is now part of my very biology.
Though I only present
as one person to the world,
I am an army.

I am a family.

People with Dissociative Identity Disorder
have resilient brains
that learned to survive situations
that should not
      be able
        to be survived.

The fight or flight.
I did both,
with varying degrees of success.
But more or less,
I learned to flee inside myself.

We never formed a
single identity,
because we were
too diverse.

        I adored my mom when
        other parts
        despised her.

            Those identities could not integrate,
            so they diverged.

I am divergence
in multitudes.

        A part loved
        my abuser
        while I hated him.

            We could not make those things come
            together as one.
            So we never did.

I lived in a state of multiplicity all my life.

And I had stern, protective parts
who hid myself from me
very skillfully.
        To be hidden was to be safe.

I wrote this book
for attention,
because children who are harmed
need all the attention
they can get.
They need to be safe
not being hidden.

I am a writer of fiction
but this is not fiction.
This is true:

I have D.I.D.
And I'm okay.

Author's Afterword

My System

I am a System of many parts. I've counted them several times (usually once a year when insurance requires an update) but mostly I don't worry about numbers. I spend my time and energy showing respect to my parts and helping them feel safe and secure. We do not always agree on everything, but we do work hard to exist peacefully.

My System is complex and diverse. My parts span from adults who are ageless all the way down to a couple toddlers and an infant. Most of my parts are children between 4 and 6 years old. The majority of child-parts are six years old and hold vast trauma from their cult experiences. I also have many adult parts.

At one time, we were all very rigid in our roles and how we interacted with one another. Since we started working together, roles have shifted, blurred, and changed. Responsibilities have altered. For instance, keeping the fact that we have DID silent and hidden was a full-time, exhausting job for many parts while I was growing up. Since I was diagnosed and decided to be open about my System, the need to hide has not been as important. Now, caring for and reparenting child parts is most essential.

Me and my parts use lots of strategies and skills to coexist peacefully. We have learned to communicate well. We have a "The body belongs to everyone" rule that means all parts are welcome to be at the "front" and pursue interests or friendships in the world.

The truth is, we are one human, but we are MANY different people. Collectively, we liked to be referred to as the Et Al System.

System Responsibility

There is a principle we (and most diagnosed multiples) live by called "System Responsibility." It means that we recognize the impact one part can have on every other part, and on other people. If one of my parts says something unkind to a friend or stranger, *I* will apologize for it as soon as I'm made aware. This can be very difficult sometimes. It would be very easy to say, "But it wasn't me, it was Alyss!" While true internally, the impact on the world is the same no matter which part did the actual deed. I will always take responsibility for what I do, even if it was a different part of myself "driving the bus."

Some of my parts *are* very angry (about the abuse, or therapy, or the fact that I even admit I have DID) and can be unkind. But not outwardly. The world is never in danger of earning the wrath of even my angriest parts. They target each other. None of my parts has ever hurt anyone else physically (except that smarmy guy we punched at the club once, but *he* knows what he did), has never been abusive, or intentionally harmful to anyone else.

"Homicidal Parts" are a lazy, overworked, and highly damaging trope used in movies and books, and is not based on reality.

Nichole Willden Et Al

Even though this memoir is written under my name, it was collectively written by Et Al.

Some of my parts gave permission for their internal names to be used in this work: Evelyn, Lily, Sadie, Beth, Rachel, Alyss, Collum, and myself Nichole. Some parts did not want to be named, so they may be included but not named, or may have been given a different name. A few asked to have their experiences included but lumped in with someone else's. Some parts did not want to be included at all, and I have honored that wish.

I must acknowledge that without *all* parts, the story is not complete. I tried to tell everything that tied together and ended neatly, but my reality includes many more rites, abuses, and situations that I did not begin to delve into in this work. Most notably, parts who have information about travel to and from the Temple have chosen not to share their experiences. When other parts are ready to tell their story, we may write another book.

Memory

I know and admit that memory is flawed. Memory retrieval can and has harmed many people and families. *I did not undergo memory retrieval* at any time during therapy. Instead, I had long-buried parts come forward and share things they remembered that I did not. When they are

110

in executive control of the body, their memories are as sound as my own.

This written account is true to the best of my knowledge and memory. Having admitted that memory is flawed, and that I might not recall everything with perfect accuracy or clarity, I can assure you that I only recounted things I remembered, without embellishment. Whether they were accurate portrayals or not, I leave to the spirit realm to determine.

I do sometimes recall things that seem or *are* impossible—monsters, talking lampposts, a dock with blood running over it—and I have to assume my childhood mind filled in the blanks with imaginary things when it could not face reality. For this memoir, I only included things that fit in the real world. This does not mean there were no monsters or blood. The parts who have those memories deserve the honor of belief and compassion as well. It only means I kept those pieces out of the memoir because I suspect my imagination filled in the blanks. I wanted this story to be as accurate to my lived experience as possible. Though, as I said before, the book is based on memory, and I admit it may be flawed.

What happened to me happened. It was real. I was abused and trafficked. That is not in question. I only bring up the flaws of memory because every detail, (like times, locations, specific wording) may be remembered a little differently by different people and parts.

Therapy

I highly recommend therapy to everyone! It has saved my life and my sanity. I started therapy because I was unhappy and suicidal. I was looking for help. Other parts came forward in therapy—some to get help, others to sabotage, depending on their reason for existence and their mood at the time—and those events happened without my knowledge or memory.

I was in therapy off-and-on for a couple decades before I got settled with a patient, wonderful therapist. In her office, I felt safest. I began to express who I was and admit to confusion and problems I never let myself share before. I told her about voices I could sometimes *hear* in my mind. All different voices: different ages, tones, depths. I told her about losing time sometimes. I told her about people calling me by other names—people I did not know. And I told her about the one voice I could always hear, my constant companion, my "Are you okay" champion.

I don't know how long my therapist knew I had DID before she diagnosed me (when Alyss came forward and admitted that she was a whole other person), but after my diagnosis, I was able to start healing. It was and still is a painful, difficult process. It requires me to acknowledge and make space for every part of me. Since those parts hold many horrific traumas, I have had to learn to feel my feelings and grieve my past.

I could never have made it this far without my trauma therapists, all of whom are represented in this narrative. They also have all done tests and separately diagnosed me with Dissociative Identity Disorder. Even when I doubt my own brain, my therapist is always there with their therapeutic protocols, tests, and patience. They guide me back to trusting myself, compassion for my parts, and acceptance of my abilities and limitations.

The Cult

I was in an underground pedophilic cult when I was a child. The dates are unclear, because many different parts of me hold different experiences in the Temple, and I cannot yet piece together a timeline from what they've shared.

What I know is that it happened in the late 1980s in a residential neighborhood somewhere in Salt Lake County, Utah. The rites and experiences described in this text happened in a basement I called the "Temple," though other parts called it "The Basement," "The Place," "The Priesthood Rooms," or "the Endowment Rooms." I suspect, based on a few details I can remember vividly, it was just the lower level of a split-level house up the street from my own.

No matter the confusion about specific details, this truth is universal across the system: I was in a cult. I was recruited out of church and the neighborhood where I played. My friend's parents were most certainly part of the underground group and may even have been running it.

I was indoctrinated to believe that I was doing a specific service in the name of God. At this time, the Et Al System is not ready to expound upon the doctrines of the Holy Josephic Priesthood. The purpose of this memoir is to share my story as a survivor of child trafficking.

I was trafficked and abused by many men and at least one woman. I was also tortured and terrified. Many methods were used as tools to secure my silence. For instance, there is debate in the System as to whether the Highest Priest was *trying* to create "multiple personalities" as a method of control and silencing. I personally think the naming and blessing process accounts for his tendency to call us by different names and assign different personality traits to us. However, this was happening during a time when there was some government experimentation to deliberately break the mind into parts. And based on a tattoo the Highest Priest had on his leg, I have reason to believe he was ex-military. I admit he could have been trying to create parts in order to keep the abused parts out of my day-to-day life. It worked well, whether he did it on purpose or not, because the Nichole part of my System was mostly unaware of the abuses and experiences in the Temple

The Priesthood

There was some confusion in the System about certain aspects of indoctrination, abuse, names, and titles. Parts remember some things differently. What I call "The Holy Josephic Priesthood" other parts said was "The Holy Brighamic Priesthood." Several emphatically claim it was "The Priesthood of the High Order of God." I'm inclined to think abusers used different names for different reasons, rather than choose to doubt the parts who are brave enough to process and share their experiences.

"The Priesthood" has many different meanings to many different parts. As I look at the whole picture, I believe all meanings are important. I was taught that the priesthood was God's power that could be accessed by men: a special kind of masculine magic that could heal the sick and cast out devils, etc. In the Temple, many parts called the men involved "Priesthood" as a title. That could be what was expected by the men involved—to give them a little mystique and power—or it could have been a childish interpretation: "They *have* the priesthood" became "they *are* the priesthood" in the mind of an abused child. Basically, I don't know what the abusers intended, and I don't care. At the end of the day, it was all a tactic to indoctrinate, control, and abuse.

The Mormon Church

I was born and raised into the Mormon church (officially known as The Church of Jesus Christ of Latter Day Saints or LDS). I attended church on Sundays with my family. We were taught about God, and priesthood, and many other things.

If you are or ever were a Mormon, some of the rites and prayers in this memoir may sound very familiar. This is because, while the cult I was in is *not* the Mormon church, it claimed to be the "Higher Priesthood" *of that church.* Everyone who abused me in the basement of my friend's home sat in pews on Sunday in the Mormon ward building. As far as I was concerned, the abuses in the basement Temple were an extension of church to my childhood brain. On Sunday, I went to church. On other days, I went to the Temple to do the "Ordinances of the Lord." It was all one thing to me.

Church was three hours long when I was a kid and I spent two-thirds of it with strangers. In this memoir, I shared some experiences about being in church and crying because I knew abuse was going to happen *next.* This occurred regularly enough that the abuse I suffered inside Mormon ward houses was also just "church" to me.

I am not claiming the greater LDS church knew about or participated in abuse of this kind. As an adult, I can now recognize how the cult was a subsect of the church and was probably happening outside of the knowledge of most LDS members.

That being said, I do think the doctrines and philosophies espoused by the LDS church fostered an environment where abusers could flourish. A part of me did once come forward to tell LDS church leaders about abuse, and I was silenced and rebuked for it. The systematic silencing and hiding of abuse in the LDS church made it a great place for abusers to set up subsects and trafficking rings. The one I was in was not the only one that existed.

I consider the LDS church to be part of my grooming process. They taught me to respect the priesthood, to doubt my doubts, and not to question authority. They expected obedience. They normalized discomfort and pain in the name of God (I'm looking at you: Fast Sunday, trek, bishop interviews, modesty, time-intensive callings, paying tithing instead of buying groceries). They led through fear and shame while claiming it was love. I was taught that "God is Love" when at the same time told he would willingly and eternally separate me from my family if I did not do everything he said. When love was uncomfortable, shameful, and fearful, I had no reason to question the "love" I was shown by the Holy Josephic Priesthood. Or by future abusers.

The Mormon God was my first abuser.

Rites, Prayers, Scriptures

The words I heard in church on Sunday were the same types of words I heard in the cult. I'm sure this was intentional on the part of the abusers. Or maybe, they truly believed they were a higher priesthood doing the will of God. But I doubt that seriously.

In the cult, they read to me from scripture. Maybe those were different texts than the ones used in church and in my home scripture study. I don't know. They were all "scriptures" to me.

The prayers sounded the same, too. "By the power of the Priesthood which I hold" was in every blessing I ever received, and at both my baptisms. Yes, both. I was baptized in a church building by the Highest Priest when I was six years old. Then again by my father at the age of accountability, two years later. That second time, I got presents and all my friends and family got to come. The first baptism was "too sacred" for presents and friends.

There are many rites I went through that are not depicted in this memoir. Some of them bear striking resemblance to ordinances in LDS Temples. I did not share everything because it was not all necessary to tell the story. Every abusive thing they did to me was tangled up with some kind of prayer, scripture, or ordinance. Even the burning of the dollhouse began with a prayer and scripture I chose not to include in the text. I also did not mention the clothing, symbols, and gestures that resemble Mormon practices, though they were part of my experience.

Because I knew the content of my memoir was heavy, I chose brevity over completeness.

Crimes and Prosecution

I am sharing my story in 2024 after almost a decade in constant, uninterrupted therapy. It has taken me a long time to cope with my diagnosis, accept my parts, build a teamwork rapport with my System, and process some of my trauma. As more and more parts get comfortable enough to go to therapy and process their trauma, my memories fill in. What I'm saying is, we are only *now* putting together the whole story of our abuse experiences, more than thirty years after the events. I have not reported these crimes.

To my knowledge, none of the people who harmed me were ever convicted or even charged. My focus has never been on prosecution, but rather on getting the help I needed to survive. They broke me, but it is *my* responsibility to fix me: one of the bitter truths of abuse survival.

I don't know if this cult is still in existence. I *do* know it did not exist solely in that single neighborhood where I was abused. It was connected to other groups or branches. My family moved to a new neighborhood when I was a small child—away from the Temple—and I was still accessed by other members of the Priesthood. I never went back to the Temple again. Instead, the abuse happened at church, usually in a small room with no windows that locked from the inside.

The abuse continued in the church building until my family moved out of state. I don't know the extent of the cult's reach. I may have moved away from their power, or I may simply have aged out of their disgusting preferences.

Searching for Answers

Recently, I started looking for more information about the cult. It has been difficult since, as far as I know, the cult did not have a name. If it did, I was never privy to that information. My experiences also took place in a time when there were not computers in every pocket or even in every home. It was easier for the abusers to hide.

Using everything my parts remember, I have searched tirelessly. I found nothing concrete yet. We heard whispers in online spaces of people who had similar experiences but have only ever had one conversation with another survivor. Their experience happened in a completely different decade and may or may not be associated with my same cult. "Higher Priesthood" was the common thread that helped us find one another.

It is my hope that other survivors will see themselves in my memoir and realize they are not alone. I *know* other children were involved. I saw them in the Temple, I heard their cries, and I was forced to harm them (and they me) at the will of the Priesthood. There are other survivors out there who, maybe like me, are only now piecing everything together.

If you survived something like this, I welcome you to contact me in my social media spaces @NicholeMWillden or to email me at outreach@nicholemwillden.com. I know there are more of us. Let my voice help yours be heard.

Human Trafficking

Human trafficking is real. It's ugly. And it's right here where you live. It's happening in your city and possibly even your neighborhood. I wrote this memoir in the hope that more people will understand the extent of the problem. People have been commodified and as long as there's a market for it, people will be bought, sold, and traded.

Please help! If you suspect something, say something. There are a lot of myths out there about trafficking—what it means and what it looks like. The truth is, I was trafficked in my own neighborhood, right under the noses of my teachers, family, and friends. Trafficking is real. Admitting that is the first step to helping end it.

My Family

I will not discuss my family of origin. I will not engage in speculation, gossip, or discourse about their involvement in my abuse. I know a lot of people are curious about what, if anything, my parents knew. I know people want to know if my siblings were also trafficked. I know the few depictions of my family in this work are not highly flattering. I know I did not share the lovely, beautiful, and sacred memories of them that I have. What I will say is this: abuse can happen to anyone at any time.

I invite the public to give my family the benefit of doubt.

To My Abusers

Don't get your hopes up that I forgot your face, your name, or other details about you. I remember you. A part of me remembers. If you thought DID was a great shield for you, I get the satisfaction of telling you it's not. All it did was lock the parts who knew about you and your crimes deep inside me. As a result, their memory is as clear as the day they were abused. We survived, and now we're talking about it. Your priesthood, your god, your name, your face, and your crimes are not sacred. I remember what you did, and I am going to tell the world.

My Happily Ever After

For those people who are worried or wondering about me and my life, I would like to share my happily ever after. The memoir ends at the beginning of the good part.

I credit my survival to a few things:

1) One is therapy. As I already said, therapy saved my life. It also taught me how to feel my feelings, accept joy, reclaim ownership of my body and my sexuality, and set boundaries. Having high-quality, compassionate, trauma-informed therapists was a game changer for me! I truly believe that without therapy I would be a suicide statistic.

2) The next thing is DID. It's kind of strange to be grateful to a mental disorder for survival, but I am. I believe I was insulated by DID. It allowed me to live a seemingly "normal" life in which I pursued an education, career, friendships, and relationships. The pain and horror of my past intruded, of course, in the form of switches, lost time, flashbacks, and other uncomfortable experiences.

I never went to substance abuse or risky behaviors to help cope with my trauma because my brain pulled me away from my discomfort or pain and deposited a different part to live through that instead. (My parts are not all as grateful for this as I have been, of course.)

The abuse created the DID, and I'm certainly not grateful for the abuse. But my brain is resilient and brilliant, and I am grateful for that every day.

3) Third is writing! I started writing intently when I was finally free from the regular abuse of the cult. I wrote fiction, but I always explored the darker sides of the human mind. At the age of 11, I wrote a book about a girl abused in a boarding school, who got out of it through magic and sass.

My emotions became words so easily to me that I often turned to writing when I experienced confusion, switches, or flashbacks. Fiction carried me through the second-hardest parts of my life and still sustains me today.

4) Finally, I get to share the beautiful happy ending my story deserves. My best friend in this memoir, the one who encouraged me and stood by my side when I was diagnosed, was my roommate at the time of my diagnosis. She met parts as they willingly came out of hiding. She developed individual friendships with many of them. They created inside jokes, laughed, and played together.

About six months after I was diagnosed, my best friend told me she had feelings for me. And not just me, some of my other parts too. We started dating even though we were living together in the same apartment already. Since we knew each other well, our relationship moved quickly. I asked her to marry me four months after we started dating. We were married seven months later.

When I was first diagnosed, I thought my life was over! I did not think anyone would love me or be able to cope with the uncertainty of life with a multiple. Instead, I earned the love and respect of a resilient, compassionate, talented, smart, and supportive human! She is my world! Every single part in my system adores her and has their own special relationship with her. And every part is her favorite part; just ask them!

Therapy, DID, and writing helped me survive. Amber is how I learned to thrive.

Doctor's Afterword

The following information was provided by a psychologist I have worked with and who has been trained and certified in treating dissociative disorders through the International Society for the Study of Trauma and Dissociation (ISSTD) who has asked to remain anonymous.

Dissociative Identity Disorder Information and Myths

What is DID?

Dissociative identity disorder (DID) is the disorder that was previously recognized as multiple personality disorder. It's characterized by the presence of two or more dissociated self states, known as alters or parts, that have the ability to take executive control and are associated with some degree of inter-identity amnesia. DID is caused by long-term childhood trauma, most frequently child abuse or neglect, that is often combined with disorganized attachment or other attachment disturbances, and is highly associated with posttraumatic stress disorder.

DID cannot form after ages 6-9 because individuals older than these ages have an integrated self identity and history. Trauma later in life can lead to posttraumatic stress disorder or complex posttraumatic stress disorder, other dissociative disorders including other specified dissociative disorder, somatic symptom disorders, or possibly borderline personality disorder, but DID requires an unintegrated mind to form.

Prevalence

DID is not rare, it is rarely caught. It is frequently claimed that DID is a uniquely rare disorder. However, when comparing DSM (The Diagnostic and Statistical Manual of Mental Disorders) prevalence rates, this is simply not true. If a prevalence rate of 1.5% is accepted for DID, it is comparable to DSM chronic major depressive disorder (1.5%), DSM bulimia nervosa in women (0.46%-1.5%), and obsessive compulsive disorder (1.1%-1.8%). The number of DID diagnoses are on the rise, primarily because 1) mental health services are becoming more accessible and socially acceptable and 2) the amount of those who experienced childhood trauma are increasing.

Origins

DID has a history of being mistaken for possession. After such a view was no longer acceptable, those with DID were seen as hysterics. Hysteria was seen as primarily dissociative in nature and could involve disturbances of memory, consciousness, affect, identity, and body functions, the same symptoms today associated with dissociative disorders and particularly with dissociative identity disorder.

The first cases in history thought to meet present day criteria for DID include:
1. The Case of Jeanne Fery - 1584
2. The Case of Sister Benedetta - 1623
3, The Case of Louis Auguste Vivet - 1882

Prognosis

With proper treatment, people with dissociative identity disorder (DID) can improve their ability to function and live fulfilling lives. Treatment often involves psychotherapy from mental health providers who are trained in trauma and dissociation. Therapy can help people process trauma, integrate their fractured selves, and cope with future distress.

However, some patients respond slowly to treatment and may need long-term supportive care. Without treatment or an accurate diagnosis, the prognosis for DID is poor. DID is often misdiagnosed later in life, and patients may be treated with medications or therapies that don't address DID directly. Additionally, DID patients often have other conditions, such as substance use disorders, anxiety, or somatoform disorders, that may go undiagnosed. Holistic clinical evaluations are necessary to treat all aspects of a patient's health.

DID has one of the most hopeful prognosis in the entire DSM as it is the only disorder that has the capacity to be completely cured. Whereas other illnesses such as anxiety or depression are often considered relapsing and remitting diseases, once an individual with DID has integrated their separate parts (if that is what is chosen), they cannot un-integrate.

Common Myths and Misperceptions

MYTH: DID IS ONLY ABOUT HAVING MULTIPLE PERSONALITIES

FACT: While alters are the best known symptom of this disorder, they aren't the only or even necessarily the main symptom. Because DID is the result of trauma, it's highly comorbid with posttraumatic stress disorder (PTSD), complex posttraumatic stress disorder (C-PTSD), flashbacks, emotional numbing, nightmares, emotional dysregulation, and pessimism about the future. Individuals with DID often have other comorbid disorders as well.

MYTH: ALTERS ARE JUST EGO STATES/MOODS WITH NAMES ATTACHED/IMAGINARY FRIENDS

FACT: Alters are dissociated self states that can be highly differentiated from each other. They can have unique names, ages, gender identities, sexualities, memories, skills, abilities, and ways of viewing and interacting with the world. Alters can even perceive themselves as different species or as members of a different race or ethnicity.

MYTH: INDIVIDUALS WITH DID ARE NEVER AWARE THEY HAVE ALTERS

FACT: It is common for individuals with DID to have awareness of their alters, to hear their alters communicating, and to have knowledge of at least some of their alters' activities. Many individuals with DID have been aware of signs of their alters since their childhood. They may once have known that they contained other "people" or known their alters personally but may have begun to ignore, forget, or reject this knowledge as they became older and realized that having alters isn't "normal."

MYTH: INDIVIDUALS WITH DID ARE NEVER AWARE OF WHAT THEIR ALTERS ARE DOING AND CANNOT COMMUNICATE WITH THEM

FACT: While all individuals with DID experience some degree of amnesia towards their alters, many can remain co-conscious with at least some of their alters. Co-consciousness is the ability for two or more alters to remain aware of each other or the outside world at the same time.

MYTH: DID IS OBVIOUS TO NOTICE IN THOSE WHO HAVE IT

FACT: Only 5-6% of those with DID are overtly inflicted with the disorder. The other 94-95% cannot be casually identified as having the disorder. Individuals who have DID are more likely to be thought to have mood disorders, personality disorders, psychotic disorders or other dissociative disorders.

MYTH: DID IS ONLY CAUSED BY SEVERE CHILD ABUSE

FACT: DID is caused by long term or repeated childhood trauma. Child abuse fits this criteria and is the most common cause of DID, with around 90% of individuals with DID having experienced child abuse or neglect. However, other forms of childhood trauma that are associated with DID include repeated medical and surgical procedures, war, human trafficking, and terrorism.

MYTH: DID IS CAUSED BY THERAPISTS/THE MEDIA/ THINKING ONESELF INTO IT

FACT: There is an abundance of evidence that supports that DID is due to long term or repeated childhood trauma. Research supports that iatrogenic/sociocognitive DID (DID resulting from therapeutic or social influences) is not the same as genuine DID.

MYTH: DID IS INCREDIBLY RARE

FACT: Between 0.1% and 2% of the population has DID. The DSM-5 places this prevalence at 1.5%. That's almost 3.2 million Americans, 0.65 million citizens of the United Kingdom, or 71 million people worldwide.

MYTH: DID IS AN AMERICAN PHENOMENON

FACT: DID has been found in all of the countries in which it has been sought, and some very forward-thinking research regarding DID comes from the Netherlands, Turkey, Puerto Rico, and New Zealand.

MYTH: DID DIDN'T EXIST BEFORE SYBIL

FACT: The first known case of DID was that of Jeanne Fery in 1584. Sybil brought awareness to DID and so allowed for an increasing number of diagnoses to be made as more funding went towards DID education and research, but DID did not begin with Sybil (nor with Eve, who came before Sybil).

MYTH: DID IS EASY TO FAKE OR IS OFTEN FAKED

FACT: While non-professionals may not be able to distinguish between those who do and do not truly have DID, professionals are trained to recognize the difference between DID and disorders that may present similarly (such as C-PTSD or BPD) or between DID and factitious disorders or malingering. It must be noted that DID is not faked at exceptionally high rates. Studies have found rates of factitious or malingered dissociative disorders to be between 2% and 14%, while malingering in other disorders range from 7%-18%.

MYTH: DID CAN FORM IN ADULTS

FACT: DID cannot form in an individual who has a fully integrated personality, and chronic childhood trauma is necessary to disrupt normal personality development. It is generally accepted that this must occur before ages 6 to 9. Age 6 is considered a critical period for the integration of one's sense of self and self history because of the maturation of the hippocampus and prefrontal cortices at this time

MYTH: THOSE WITH DID CAN CHOOSE TO GET RID OF OR IMMEDIATELY INTEGRATE ALTERS

FACT: Alters are dissociated parts of the self. They cannot be gotten rid of or killed any more than one's traits, flaws, or other mental health symptoms can be magically gotten rid of or cured. Unfortunately, unlike many other mental health conditions, DID cannot be treated by medication.

MYTH: THOSE WITH DID ARE DANGEROUS KILLERS

FACT: Like other mentally ill populations, those with DID are no more likely to be dangerous or abusive than anyone else. However, DID forms because of chronic childhood trauma, and individuals with DID are highly likely to be re-traumatized and be victims of further abuse and violence. Contrary to popular belief, it's extremely uncommon for those with DID to have an "evil" or physically violent alter.

If a person with DID does have an "evil" or violent part, the risk is to the person with DID, not the public.

Acknowledgments

The creation of this book could not have been possible without many amazing people. Your name on the acknowledgments page is not enough for how much you impacted my life, but you deserve to know you changed my life for the better.

First, I need to thank my therapists! Thank you, thank you, thank you! My life and my peace of mind are due to your diligence. Thank you for putting up with the eye rolling, muttering, and sass. Thank you for sitting in the sadness, heartbreak, and devastation with me. Thank you for boundaries, strategies, skills, and laughter. Thank you for crisis calls and extra sessions. Thank you for seeing all the parts of me without judgment. Thank you for calling me out on my shit and seeing when I'm tapping. You are the front line in the war of mental illness, and that means you're brave, creative, and endlessly brilliant.

Thank you, Hilary. Without you and your patience, I would never have been brave enough to put all this into words. There are a thousand things I want to say to you, but this is the most important one: I found safety in the space you created for me. Thank you for believing me and believing in me.

Thank you, Kami! I am still kicking ass and taking names. But you knew that because I'm a badass, obvi.

Thank you, Deborah. The army you created may be small, but it is mighty!

Thank you so much to my Beta Team! I had many of you help me shape my messages into a better, more understandable form. And your questions helped shape the Afterword of this book. Thank you especially to Haley Kelley (you know!), Emma Sturdevant, and Amber Adams.

I could never have made this book what it is without my excellent editor, Misty Bourne! Thank you for helping me be brave and trusting. You took the story of a terrified author and helped it shine its brightest, while gently soothing the terror away. And I'm not sure you even know how much you helped me.

Other people who had big impact and probably don't know it: Jamie, Samantha Gibb, Sandi Barnhurst, McCall Davis, Amy Kunz, Krystal (at the front desk), Deborah Christensen, Joshua, Kali and Golden, Deb Parr, Adam, the late DJ Turnley, David and Jeanne, the late Casi DiCamillo, Amelia Anderson, Julie Larson, and Jennifer McCullough.

I would also love to thank the student therapists in Springfield, Missouri, who helped me survive my 20s. That's when I first started having flashbacks and suicidal depression. I do not remember your names, sadly. Some of you worked very hard to help me in the early 2000s. A tag-team duo of you were the first ones to push me into staying in therapy when I started to "get better." You noticed a pattern of quitting therapy and you called me out on it. As a result, you got some parts to come see you who never went to therapy before. You did not know they were dissociated parts, but you helped them. I especially wish I could thank the therapist who encouraged critical thinking about some of the teachings of my church even though I pushed back hard and shut you down. You were also the therapist who I had to leave abruptly when I moved away to Utah. Your impact on my life is so much bigger than you could ever know.

Thank you to Potion. I know you can't read this because you're a dog. I mean, you're a super smart service dog, so I wouldn't be surprised if you learned how to read. But you're also scared of feathers, so... You have helped me find my way back to safety countless times when I fell into darkness and pain.

Thank you to Kathy and Mark. You love me like I'm yours, and that's uncomfortable and confusing for me a lot. But it's also beautiful. Kathy, you are a hero in my life story in ways you may not ever know.

Amber. If I listed all the ways, there would not be enough pages or words. Thank you for loving every broken piece of me. Thank you for sitting with me when the pain hits. Thank you for holding my hand during flashbacks. Thank you for singing "Wants a Slurpee" and "Itsy Bitsy Spider." Thank you for playing with ponies and making spider pancakes. Thank you for not knowing anything about Hilly's Heroes. Thank you for your worship of brownies, your obsession with Zest, and your dream (you know the one). Thank you for ocean waves, Redwoods, and Disney vacations. Thank you for Nobnie. Thank you for Cookie Club! Thank you for being the Nik to my Nia, the Scott to my Emma, and the raised brow to my bratty backtalk. Thank you for magic. Thank you for tattoos. Thank you for learning to publish, for reading reviews instead of me, and doing the icky parts. Thank you for formatting, learning graphic design, starting my mailing list, building websites, and proofreading all the things. Thank you for gasping, crying, and laughing in all the right places. Thank you for bringing meals to my hands when I'm on a writing sprint. Thank you for believing I'm not the [REDACTED] I always self-diagnose. Thanks for always seeing me when no one else can or does. Thank you especially for walking by my side while we write our life into existence. I love you more.

Also by Nichole M. Willden

The Guild Series

No one joins a cult on purpose.

Emma doesn't remember how she got to the Guild. No one will tell her. The only thing her superiors ever say is "Be Obedient."

Emma is done with Obedience. She wants a life: friends, a boyfriend, and a family who loves her. But being in the Guild is not a choice. It's a life sentence. When Emma begins to rebel against the rules, Leader tightens his hold. The Guilded cage he created crashes down, forcing her to make a choice: stay and obey, or fight to get free of his far-reaching authority.

No one joins a cult on purpose, but getting out requires a strategy.

Let's Stay in Touch!

Get updates and freebies by signing up for my newsletter at
www.nicholemwillden.com
Follow me on social media @nicholemwillden.

About the Author

Nichole M. Willden is a poet, writer, and author of The Guild series. A survivor of indoctrination and abuse, Nichole has spent decades writing fiction that sizzles with themes of enslavement, hope, and resilience. Nichole lives and writes in the Rocky Mountains with her wife, who is helpful to the writing process, and their puppy, Potion, who is delightfully unhelpful.

www.ingramcontent.com/pod-product-compliance
Lightning Source LLC
Chambersburg PA
CBHW071157120626
46546CB00006B/2311